Immaculate Emotions

Alta Newlun

Immaculate Emotions
Copyright © 2023 by Alta Newlun

ISBN: 978-1639457427 (sc)
ISBN: 978-1639457434 (e)

All rights reserved. No part of this publication may be reproduced, distributed, or transmitted in any form or by any means, including photocopying, recording, or other electronic or mechanical methods, without the prior written permission of the publisher, except in the case brief quotations embodied in critical reviews and other noncommercial uses permitted by copyright law.

The views expressed in this book are solely those of the author and do not necessarily reflect the views of the publisher, and the publisher hereby disclaims any responsibility for them.

Writers' Branding
(877) 608-6550
www.writersbranding.com
media@writersbranding.com

Readers Notes

This book is to all of those who believed in me.
It's been a long year for me.
It has been a challenge for me to finish.
But it is done!!!!!!!

Love all of you.

Alta Newlun
September 6, 2009

Note to My People

This is to everybody that truly believed in me!

I love you and your strong arms. You guys mean so much to me.

You have been there when I needed you so.

Alta Newlun

Table of Contents

Times of Tears 1
I Believed in You 2
Love Is to Let Go 3
The Birdy That Flew Away 4
Hard Time Got Harder 5
Finding Happier Days 6
My Million in Gold 7
Two Hearts Torn Apart 8
My Forgotten Day 9
Tears of Hurtfulness 10
My Night and Day 11
Struggling Times 12
Flowered Seed 13
Missing Souls 14
Don't Ask Why? 15
Crushed and Broken 16

Only Time	17
Bottom of Your Line	18
Silenced and Misunderstood	19
Only to Communicate	20
I Am Difficult, You Won't Understand	21
Crying Alone	22
To My Disappointments	23
My Silence	24
Brown Eyes	25
Tears and Heartaches	26
Eugene	27
Days Can Be Peaceful	28
Life As a Bird	29
Birds Are Beautiful Creatures	30
Loving Rose	31
To Hear Birds Sing	32
Hurting Tears	33
My Beatless Heart	34
My Big Bear	35
Our Troubled Times	36
Real Tears	37
My Hopes and Dreams	38
Finding Your Happiness	39

My Sadness 40
Clouds of Tears 41
Finding a Happy Present 42
Finding My Sunshine 43
Different Dreams 44
A Million in Happiness 45
Loving Life 46
Is Our Love from Your Heart? 47
Not Time Yet 48
Friends 49
Valuable As a Brick of Gold 50
Eyes and Ears 51
Good Bye to You 52
Missing Souls 53
Don't Ask Why 54
Meanless Words 55
Only to Your Sorrows 56
Beyond the Skies 57
Sweet Happiness 58
Love That Grows 59
Peaceful Sky 60
Peeking Sun 61
Selfish One 62

Birds..63

All Creations 64

Happiness is Within You 65

Blessed with Imagination.....................66

The Beholder, Beyond the Clouds........67

Respect Yourself 68

My Love Letter....................................69

Does He Know? Probably Not!............70

My Mirror..71

My Biggest Stranger Eugene 72

I Am Twisted and Tangled 73

My Question?......................................74

It Rains for My Pain 75

Looking Towards Your Dreams............76

Pain and Destruction...........................77

That Kinda Love 78

Here's to My Past.................................79

To Wayne 80

My Misunderstood Soul......................81

Lifes Vacation......................................82

Eugene 83

My Sweet Ninnie.................................84

At Home 86

Eyes of the Disabled	88
Why Can't We	89
Look Inside My Heart	90
My Meaning	91
Grow Seasons	92
In My Tears	93
Lost And Hurt	94
Dying Flowers	95
Stormy Clouds	96
Storms Together	97
It's All Good	98
Weather That Is Good	99
Love Is Like a Flower	100
The Storms of the Day	101
To My Selfish One	102
Rainbow of Storms	103
Raindrops of Tears	104
Days of Clouds	105
To My Readers	106

Immaculate Emotions

Times of Tears

All the time I cried for you. All tears I had for you…are faded in the wind. But, now your gone there are smiles again.

Alta Newlun

I Believed in You

All the times I believed in you.
All the times you let me down.
All the times I cried for you without a sound.
I kept hoping and praying, that things
would change but it never did. Did it!!!!!

Immaculate Emotions

Love Is to Let Go

To truly love is to let go, and cry and worry from afar. But have Faith that you taught them well. And always pray for Angels to watch over them when you can't.

Alta Newlun

The Birdy That Flew Away

To my bird that left my nest. So young and free always independent, so young and free. Did you see your momma, did you watch her? Did you even learn? My little birdie so young, so free.

Hard Time Got Harder

It seemed hard times got harder. Bad times got worse, there was never a change. Just tears of hurt. Clouds of tears; that always came my way.

Alta Newlun

Finding Happier Days

My piece of mind is worth a million, now your gone. My pain of your screams and fights; are slowly leaving me. Know I will find happy days to come.

My Million in Gold

Real love is like gold you should always cherish it. Hugs and kisses are worth a million too. Some day I hope to find my million in GOLD.

Alta Newlun

Two Hearts Torn Apart

Two hearts torn apart never to be one again. My heart is torn apart filled with clouds of tears. Never to be heard by you again. But I still wish you well.

My Forgotten Day

Forgotten and unrepresented, forgotten to be loved. Time invested loving you and only to be forgotten, on my special day of the year. Just to have memories of watching you grow to be men. I love you guys. But only not to be returned. Happy Mother's Day guys!

Tears of Hurtfulness

Our arguments became painful and destructive. You cause me tears and hurtfulness. Just leaving to wonder why all my time and caring became nothing at all. You say you love me and care for me. But you are never there for me.

My Night and Day

Even when I feel so alone. I try and try but still you don't know how to hear me. And, I feel so empty and alone. I just now how to rain tears from my eyes for you. It just seems there is no getting through to you. We are like night and day with no sunshine to warm us up. But still I miss you when your not there.

Alta Newlun

Struggling Times

Life seem such a struggle with difficult times.
Hunger and death seem common around me. There
is no sunshine but tears to fill the world today.

Immaculate Emotions

Flowered Seed

To my flowered seed. I spent a lifetime watching you grow. To be big and beautiful. But now it's time for you to blossom on your own; even if it means watch you weight at times.

Missing Souls

Two souls that can't touch each other. Not even in passing. One jealous and angry. The other broken and disappointed. No matter how much she tries to touch his soul she seems to miss. While he seems to crush her. She tears up and wonders why.

Immaculate Emotions

Don't Ask Why?

I hear you are not supposed to ask why?
Why things happen the way they do. But I sure do.
When I know I tried so hard to get through to you.
Why do you refuse to hear me! It seems all I
hear from you is the same song over and over!

Alta Newlun

Crushed and Broken

Are broken hearts meant to be? Mended,
tattered and torn. Do hearts bleed
or do they cry in your sleep?

Can hearts break so many times they just
can't mend themselves any more?

What happens to a crushed and broken
heart? Does it wither and die like an old
rose that nobody wants anymore?

Crushed and broken, old and withered. Does
anybody feel for an old broken heart? Can
time stitch and old torn heart? Or does it
cry at night from all the pain endured.

Only Time

What time has when your tired and weathered. Time just disappoints you, cause tears and heart ache.

When you try and try but noting changes. But your mind! I guess that is why they say time will tell. It only tells the truth. If only your eyes can see.

That can only be time!

Alta Newlun

Bottom of Your Line

Standing last on your list and damned near forgotten. If this is love to you then,
NO THANK YOU!
Standing last on your list and always forgotten!

Silenced and Misunderstood

Silenced by the one who refused to hear.
Misunderstood by the one who just doesn't
Care.

Would they be missed?
OR
Misunderstood?

Would they be loved or be hated?

Alta Newlun

Only to Communicate

I try to communicate but you say it's fighting. I try to make you understand me but you just say why can't you get along. But what you don't know is I feel the same. I don't understand why talking is so hard for you and me. When I have so much to say with nobody to hear me.

I Am Difficult, You Won't Understand

You say I am difficult. I think you just don't care. You say why can't we get along. But to me it means, to never be as close as I want you to be. It means so much to me for you to understand me. To truly hear me. I want you to feel my tears. But somehow I know that is not possible; but I still have Hope.

Crying Alone

Crying without you. We don't have time
to share. I wish you could understand me.
I feel you don't care! I wish you new how
to love me. I wish I felt you cared.

To My Disappointments

When I think of you I think of disappointments and tears. It just makes me sad, to think whatever I do or try you won't understand. Why don't you learn to be open minded. And learn to really love me. But that also means knowing really how to love.

Alta Newlun

My Silence

 Silence seems deafening when you refuse to hear me. And you sure don't have time to listen to me.

 Do you have time to care for yourself? Because you don't care for me!
 Believe me you will never be forgotten.

Brown Eyes

To my brown eyes. They seemed to make me so blue as ever. To never be understood. Never to be cared for but to be use all you think you can. My Brown Eyes never have respect for me or yourself. To love me Brown Eyes you need to love yourself.

Alta Newlun

Tears and Heartaches

What loving you means to me.

Loving you means tears and heartache.

Loving you is always to be misunderstood.

Loving you means always to be last on your list.

Loving you means unshared dreams.

Loving you means separate life plans.

Loving you means a life of disappointments.

Loving you means my heart could never be whole!

Immaculate Emotions

Eugene

What is sad is when I think of talking to you I would rather use paper and pencil. Because that is all that hears me. I now you won't.

Alta Newlun

Days Can Be Peaceful

How peaceful it is to watch the rain fall. To smell the air and to watch the birds fly by singing their beautiful songs. Knowing there would be another day to try over again. That is the best thing to have; Another Day.

Life As a Bird

Have you ever watched a bird; and wonder if only you were a bird. What would my world be like? Would things be so much simpler. Would life be much brighter. In your eyes as a bird?

Alta Newlun

Birds Are Beautiful Creatures

Birds are simple creations. They soar in the sky and live off the land. They sing beautiful songs. They are God's beautiful creatures of the land and the air.

Loving Rose

Is love to keep a rose from blossoming.
To grow in her own perfume?

Should you pick her thorn off so
she should wither and die?

Love should grow and blossom not wither and die!

Alta Newlun

To Hear Birds Sing

Love is to hear a bird sing. To watch the sun raise and the flowers grow. Their love is all around us. Only if you were to look.

Hurting Tears

I don't understand why you do the thing you do? Why can't you love me right? Why do you like hurting me the way you do? It seems I try and try but nothing really changes; but my tears for you.

Alta Newlun

My Beatless Heart

My torn soul, my crying heart; that can't remember to take a beat every day. It thinks of you and bleeds all the way.

Immaculate Emotions

My Big Bear

To my Big Bear.
So grizzly, so strong, what's going
on. Is there something wrong.

Oh, Big Bear, you don't have to be so
strong. Tell you momma what is wrong.

Our Troubled Times

We live in troubled times. Hardship and tears. What happened to kindness, loving and even compassion. What happens to I love you and it comes from your heart. And a kiss that came from your soul.

I guess that is not possible you have no heart and soul.

Immaculate Emotions

Real Tears

What happened to real tears that are true to your heart? But not crocodile those that are phony and makes us fall apart.

Alta Newlun

My Hopes and Dreams

I had such hopes and I had much dreams for us. But you tore them all apart. And you ripped them at the seams. So my dreams are all gone. Just like you.

Finding Your Happiness

I hope you find happiness, some day in your heart. And learn how not to tear people apart.

Alta Newlun

My Sadness

Jealousy, Anger, Evil and Hurt!
Was it better to take it out on me?
How does it feel to hurt as much as you hurt
Others?

Immaculate Emotions

Clouds of Tears

Rain drops are like a shower from heaven.
It's clouds of tears raining on us, washing
the old to bring up the new.
And raining clouds of tears for the unhappy ones.

Alta Newlun

Finding a Happy Present

To let go is to release the past. That
could be the happiest feeling yet.
The feeling of letting go and moving on.
The burdens of our past set free. To
find the happy present we deserve.

Immaculate Emotions

Finding My Sunshine

It seems you never wanted the
sun to shine my way.

That is why I have to leave you today.

No hugs goodbye, I refused to cry.

I know good bye is best for you and I.

Different Dreams

Our dreams were never shared. My life views your never cared. But your jealousy just made you mean and angry.

When we shared good by you have lots of anger for the world today. That is why I had to say good bye.

A Million in Happiness

Happiness is worth a million only
if you know how to find it.

Look past the ground and into
the sky to find happiness.

Alta Newlun

Loving Life

Learning to laugh at life is learning to live.

Finding joy is finding love in your true friends.

True friends are rare like real love.

Real love is forever it comes in different ways.
You just need to know how to look for it.

Is Our Love from Your Heart?

What does the word "LOVE" mean to you?

Is it from your heart or just a thing to say?
Is it real to you or something to play with?

So tell me what does love mean to you? Love should not hurt your body nor your mind. What do people do in the name of love?

Do they disrespect and call that Love?

Not Time Yet

So, it is not my time. But when will it be?

To shine in the sun. To be admired, to be someone!

Immaculate Emotions

Friends

Friends are there in good times and bad. Don't judge unless you want to be judged. Everybody has something in their closet.

Alta Newlun

Valuable As a Brick of Gold

Some people don't know what
the value of life is worth.

They don't seem to know what is
important and what is not.

Kindness, love and true understanding
is what is most important in life.

Learn to truly give a little and you get so
much in return. Caring, loving and true
understanding is worth a brick of gold.

Eyes and Ears

You can't hide from eyes and ears. You can't hide from the real truth in life.

Not even the version you made up in your mind. But the real truth that you try to hide from people. But you are not very good at it.

Alta Newlun

Good Bye to You

I say my good byes to you my love.

And I say hello to a happy heart. So my heart filled with tears and sorrow.

A hello to a better tomorrow. I can't fix our jealousy. I can't fit your sorrow. But I can have a better tomorrow.

Missing Souls

Two souls that can't touch each other. Not even in passing. One jealous and angry. The other broken and disappointed.

No matter how much she tries to touch his soul she seems to miss while he seems to crush hers. She tears up and wonders why?

Don't Ask Why

I heard your not supposed to ask why?

Why things happen the way they do. But I sure do. When I know I tried so hard to get through to you; and nothing seems to change. But my way of thinking about you. Why you refuse to hear me! It seems all I hear from you is the same song over and over!

Immaculate Emotions

Meanless Words

Kind words are nothing when they are backed with hurt and pain. Words mean nothing when you won't show me what they mean. Words are not always kind; but they always seem sharper than a two sided sword, and stabs deeper than a knife.

So you say I have inspired you. What does that mean to you? Are they words that fill a book: I know so well? Will those words bloom in the spring like sunflowers.

OR

Will they die in the heat of the summer sun?

Can you tell me that?

Only to Your Sorrows

Goodbye my weepy sorrow. In hopes for better tomorrows. Weepy tears and fears I refuse to hold for you anymore. It is time for your tears and fears to grow by the day. It is time for you to wonder why thangs are the way they turn out.

Immaculate Emotions

Beyond the Skies

Look to the heavens above and beyond the skies for true happiness from above.

Alta Newlun

Sweet Happiness

My happiness is swinging on a big swing. Closing my eyes and remembering when I was a girl. With my eyes closed, I swing higher and higher. That is my happiness.

Immaculate Emotions

Love That Grows

To love someone is to let them grow.
To step back and let them bloom.

You can love from afar; You can love close by.

But Just Love!

Peaceful Sky

Sunrise, Sunsets under the peaceful sky.

Stars rise, stars set under the same peaceful skies.

Peeking Sun

The sun peeks high up through the trees to light the evening skies. As the beautiful skies. The trees blow as wind goes by. As the evening grows older and the sun says good night.

Selfish One

I don't know why you have to be so mean just for you to feel better. What happened to respect, kindness and love. But you don't seem to know how to give that to others. you only find it for yourself.

Immaculate Emotions

Birds

If I easy a bird, where would I go? What would I see? What would I learn? Only if I was a bird!

All Creations

To see the beauty in nature, is to know the beauty of life. With all his creations.

Big and small from big sunflowers to tiny ants, learn to notice them. Then you'll learn to see the world. And all the amazing thing in it.

Happiness is Within You

Meanness and hatefulness is all you know. You have problems only you can fix.

You fix only what you want and keep what you want to. Maybe because you are happy the way you are.

Alta Newlun

Blessed with Imagination

If you are blessed with imagination, then you are truly blessed. Because it is truly golden.

The Beholder, Beyond the Clouds

My beauty, I see lies in my beholder.
That lives beyond the clouds.

Respect Yourself

To respect yourself is to truly be honest with yourself. Figure out what matters to you. And know what you want. Never wait for someone else to do it. Do if for yourself. Then it will be done right!

Real love is to truly love yourself. Look ahead, don't look back and follow your dreams. Because our worth it! Even if it is not shown by the one you love.

If you don't do it today. You won't do it tomorrow.

When do you know its time is over? When do you say enough is enough? Our show no love and no respect. Never had it and never found it and you never will! When there is no respect there will never be true love!

My Love Letter

To my love, I am writing you now because you never heard me then. But know it is just to late. I still often try but you can't hear a thing I say. To you it is a joke. You just laugh. But only in your eyes.

But like many times before I tried to tell you what my heart feels. But like always you don't know how to hear me. Or it just did not seem to matter much.

Alta Newlun

Does He Know? Probably Not!

I don't even now why I even care. I guess it is because I tried so hard to fix things. But you were not there to hear me. So I am telling you in this letter. And yes it is too late.

My Mirror

Sometimes your children seem to be a mirror of your past and present. Whether it seems right or wrong. That is how it is.

Life is a mirror, it is a reflection of what you don't want to see. Do you hide your mirror because it is to hard to see? Only you can make it better So why not do something about it; or are you happy with what you see.

Alta Newlun

My Biggest Stranger Eugene

I can know you a lifetime and you still will be
my biggest stranger I don't talk to strangers.

But I promised myself no more!

I refuse to love a stranger, and I know
that is all we would ever be.

My biggest stranger.

Immaculate Emotions

I Am Twisted and Tangled

"YOU"
Wounded my heart an twisted my soul, and tangled my mind. And you called it Love!

My Question?

Why do people cause your heart to cry? When you try so hard to love them. And all they seem to do is cause your heart much pain.

Someone explain that!

Immaculate Emotions

It Rains for My Pain

When I think of you. I see tears of rain from the skies. And each drop represents the pain you caused my soul to endure.

Just because I tried to love you.

Alta Newlun

Looking Towards Your Dreams

Life is precious, time is very limited.

Decide what is important in your life, what matters the most. Work forward to our dreams. Don't waste your time with troubles and worries. But use our time for dreams and goals. Do it today! Because you don't know how many tomorrows you have.

Pain and Destruction

Where are we today when life
has less than not value.

When Momma and Daddy don't
care for the life they made.

When life is destructible, and can be thrown away.

When pain has no heartache not tears or sorrow.

Where are we when life has no loss or value?

It seems today we are replaceable. What
does that say for the next generation.

Alta Newlun

That Kinda Love

So you say you love me?
But I just don't have time for that kind of love.

We both are growing older. Both with different dreams. I have waited a life time for my dreams.

I know now it is time to follow my dreams.

Here's to My Past

Baby here is to making you my
past. It is better left alone.

No more tears from you!
And no more song and dance!

Let's make you my past!

Do it for us or at least for me!

So here is to my past and loving my future.

To Wayne

You want be forgotten!

But I know you are in a better place and finally at Peace! With yourself.

GOD REST

A. Newlun

Footnote:

This is to my friend that died so tragically. But finally at rest. He loved to write but did not finish his dream. You will always be remembered by me!

I will miss our talks our dreams
never to be forgotten!

Immaculate Emotions

My Misunderstood Soul

To the misunderstood soul that went to heaven
What did you do? You stupid soul, they tore
you up with bricks; so no one would know you.
But we still knew you; we still loved you so.

Oh my misunderstood soul what did you do?
Who did you make mad. I will never know.

I told you to take care! I told you to
be good! But you did not listen!

But now you have gone home and nobody
will read your thoughts a or dreams.

But I will always remember you! To me you
Will never be a wasted soul.

Alta Newlun

Lifes Vacation

To see life through a child's eyes is to really enjoy
Life. To laugh and to play like a
child is the best vacation ever.

Eugene

All I know to do is pray for you. Instead of having anger for you; I will ask for understanding, and knowledge to forgive you Because I know I didn't deserve your treatment. And I will learn to go on with peace and without resentment for you.

A. Newlun

Footnote:

This is to my friend that died so tragically. But finally at rest. He loved to write but did not finish his dream. You will always be remembered by me!

I will miss our talks our dreams never to be forgotten!

Alta Newlun

My Sweet Ninnie

To a woman that taught me that love sees no color.
You will always be remembered and never forgotten.

I know someday I will see you again with
long wings and as pretty as ever.

To the ones we loved and foolishly lost. From the
good old woman to the plain just average individual.
We will always remember you; and mourn our loss.

The day we put Ninny to rest; it was the last week
in March. It was to be a beautiful Spring Day.

But there were no pretty birds,
butterflies or blue clouds.

But on the day we put Ninny to rest the
skies were crying for us who lost so much.
And what the good Lord has gained.

Immaculate Emotions

After an hour the rain turned to ice, and the grass was crunchy. The blue clouds went very dreary and dim. And on that Spring Day we all felt the LOST.

NENNIE YOU WILL ALWAYS
BE REMEMBERED

TO NINNIE

From your loving granddaughter, ERIKA!

Alta Newlun

At Home

He called me home and I took His hand.

At heaven we met, at peace we stand. I am Home happy and blessed. When God called me away from the pain and led me in the direction to walk in His name.

For I am okay so please do not grieve. I have only taken the road God has chosen for me. And if anytime you miss my face; just know that I am here and to never be erased.

My time has come and now I must go. I am happy at home, at a place where I belong.

Erika
March 23, 2009
p.s.

Immaculate Emotions

I do agree Ninny you have made a difference in my life.

I will always remember you.

From your hugs to my very favorite and cherished purple sweater too. Which I will always cherish.

From Your Loving Friend,
Alta Newlun

Alta Newlun

Eyes of the Disabled

Please don't see me by what is wrong with me. But look at what I can do. And what I have accomplished in life.

Learn my goals that I have met; learn me! I am a person too. With feelings just like you.

So before you judge me, please take time to know me.

Immaculate Emotions

Why Can't We

In the world of can not's, there is still a lot we can do. If I talk funny or just can't hear well, give me a chance be kind, I am a person too. Please look beyond what you think you know, and just know me.

A. Newlun

Footnote:

This is to my friend that died so tragically. But finally at rest. He loved to write but did not finish his dream. You will always be remembered by me!

I will miss our talks our dreams never to be forgotten!

Look Inside My Heart

Why does this world make us feel ashamed of who we are. And refuses to look in our hearts to find out the greatness of who we become.

A. Newlun

Footnote:

This is to my friend that died so tragically. But finally at rest. He loved to write but did not finish his dream. You will always be remembered by me!

I will miss our talks our dreams never to be forgotten!

Immaculate Emotions

My Meaning

From the past to the present what can we say?
To disrespect or respect what can we do?

Alta Newlun

Grow Seasons

Birds fly, flowers grow, birds sing, does flowers cry?
To hear, to see to cry isn't that what life is all about?

In My Tears

When I cry why can't you hear my tears?

When I need you why can't I feel your arms?

You say you love me, but to me it's
just a lot of tears and loneliness.

Alta Newlun

Lost And Hurt

When I am lost I can't see your eyes. When I feel alone, I never have your arms to hold me. To tell me everything is okay.

Where are you when I need you? I just don't know.

Immaculate Emotions

Dying Flowers

So you say you will buy me flowers. I have all the flowers I need. I hold them in my heart. Your flowers wither and die, like my love for you.

Alta Newlun

Stormy Clouds

The eye of the clouds seems so clear, when I am without you. But when you are near my clouds are gray and stormy. It seems I need the sun to survive. So go away and the clouds will too.

Storms Together

The wind and rain is who we are together.
But apart the sun seems to shine my way.

Alta Newlun

It's All Good

I wish you well, no harm to come to you. I hope you have all in life you are wanting to become. Some days I think of you and no regrets of our parting. I wish you well in life to come.

Weather That Is Good

Life is like weather. There is good days and bad days. Eugene I wish you more good than bad. I hope you find happiness in your world to come. Because I know I will. Soon you will be a memory.

Alta Newlun

Love Is Like a Flower

Love is like a flower. It needs to bloom
and grow. But to many storms will
make even roses wilt and die.

The Storms of the Day

Walking around in a cloud of darkness never to see the light of the sun. Storms are rolling, clouds are crying. The sun comes out and brightens your day.

Alta Newlun

To My Selfish One

My anger for you grows stronger everyday.
My walls I have built are made of stone.

You play with my feelings and don't even
care. Eugene your selfish, mean and careless.
You wonder why I grew so heartless.

Rainbow of Storms

Eugene, when I think of you, I think of dark clouds or raindrops never to see a rainbow at the end of a bad storm.

Alta Newlun

Raindrops of Tears

You're my broken heart, my tears
my sadness, and my fears.

You are even my disappointments. But soon
I will find my sunshine with no more rain.

Immaculate Emotions

Days of Clouds

On a good day or bad day you are never there. You are my clouds my storms. The rain that comes from my eyes. Eyes are blue but will soon shine again.

To My Readers

First of all I want to thank you for buying my book. This book was inspired by a really bad relationship that has been gone and lost.

This book has been a great help to me in my struggle to try to move on with my life. It has helped me to realize what is really important to me.

I hope you enjoyed reading it as much as I did writing it.

Thank you again and May God Bless You.

Alta Newlun

www.ingramcontent.com/pod-product-compliance
Lightning Source LLC
LaVergne TN
LVHW091559060526
838200LV00036B/919